GEOGRAPHY FACT FILES

MOUNTAINS

Anna Claybourne

HODDER
Wayland

an imprint of Hodder Children's Books

GEOGRAPHY FACT FILES

COASTLINES
DESERTS
MOUNTAINS
OCEANS
POLAR REGIONS
RIVERS

Produced by Monkey Puzzle Media Ltd

Gissing's Farm, Fressingfield, Suffolk IP21 5SH, UK

First published in 2004 by Hodder Wayland

An imprint of Hodder Children's Books

Text copyright © 2004 Hodder Wayland

Volume copyright © 2004 Hodder Wayland

Editor	Catherine Burch
Designer	Jamie Asher
Picture Researcher	Sally Cole
Illustrator	Michael Posen
Consultant	Michael Allaby

Printed in China

Cover picture: Grand Tetons reflecting in the water of Snake River, Wyoming, USA.

Title page picture: K2, now officially measured to be the world's second-highest mountain.

British Library Cataloguing in Publication Data

Claybourne, Anna

  Mountains. – (Geography fact files)

  1.Mountains – Juvenile literature 2.Mountain ecology – Juvenile literature

  I.Title

  551.4'32

ISBN 07502 4393 7

Acknowledgements

We are grateful to the following for permission to reproduce photographs: Alamy 19 bottom, 47; Corbis 1 (Galen Rowell), 6 (Bettmann), 9 top (Danny Lehman), 15, 17 (Galen Rowell), 27 (James A Sugar), 28 (Gunther Marx Photography), 39 bottom (Marc Muench), 40 (Dewitt Jones); Corbis Digital Stock 3 bottom inset, 33; FLPA 14 (Steve McCutcheon), 45 (David Hosking); Getty Images *front cover* (William Smithey Jr); James Davis Travel Photography 5 top, 11 top, 32, 46; Mountain Camera 19 top; Nature Picture Library *back cover left* (Konstantin Mikhailov), 22 (Konstantin Mikhailov), 25 top (Juan Manuel Borrero); NHPA 29 (T Kitchin and V Hurst); PA Photos 26 (Alison Hargreaves), 31 top (EPA); Rex Features 9 bottom (SIPA), 36 (B Veysett/SIPA), 41 (Lehtikuva Oy), 43 top (SIPA); Robert Harding Picture Library 3 middle inset (Tony Demin/International Stock), 4 (S Sassoon), 12 (Tony Waltham), 20 (Ron Sanford/International Stock), 25 bottom (Tony Waltham), 37 (E Simaner), 39 top (Tony Demin/International Stock); Still Pictures 3 top inset (Peter Weimann), 5 bottom (Roland Seitre), 11 bottom (Alain Compost), 21 top (Peter Weimann), 21 bottom (Fritz Polking), 30 (Hartmut Schwarzbach), 31 bottom (Edward Parker), 34 (John Isaac), 35 top (Adrian Arbib), 35 bottom (Mark Edwards), 38 (Chiaus Lotcher), 42 (Daniel Dancer), 43 bottom (Fritz Polking); Swift Imagery 10 (David Young), 13 (G R Park), 44.

Hodder Children's Books

A division of Hodder Headline Limited

338 Euston Road, London NW1 3BH

CONTENTS

The words that are explained in the glossary are printed in **bold** the first time they are mentioned in the text.

WHAT IS A MOUNTAIN?

Everyone knows what a mountain looks like – and yet there is no agreed definition of what a mountain really is. Most geographers (people who study the Earth) agree that a mountain is a big piece of land, with steep, sloping sides, that sticks up from the land around it. Some say that to be a true mountain, it has to be over 1,000 m high (measured from sea level). Others believe that any large, steep-sided lump of land can be called a mountain.

LOCATION FILE

HOME OF THE GODS

The ancient Greeks believed that their gods lived at the top of Mount Olympus, a 2,917 m-high mountain in the north of Greece. Many mountains around the world are regarded as sacred, including Mount Fuji in Japan and Mount Kenya in Kenya, Africa.

MOUNTAIN RANGES

Because of the way they are formed (see page 8), most mountains are found in mountain ranges. These are long chains or groups of mountains that can stretch for hundreds or even thousands of kilometres. For example, the Andes mountain range reaches all the way down the western side of South America, from Colombia in the north to Patagonia (the southern part of Chile and Argentina) in the south.

5,895 m-high Kilimanjaro, in Tanzania, East Africa, has been regarded as sacred by local people for centuries. Early explorers also thought it was magical because it had snow on top, despite being almost on the Equator.

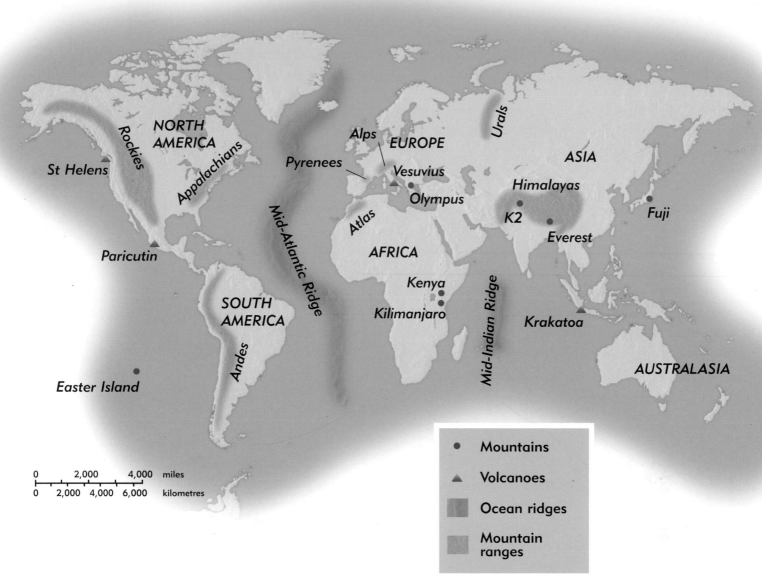

NORTH AMERICA

Rockies

St Helens

Appalachians

Paricutin

SOUTH AMERICA

Andes

Easter Island

Mid-Atlantic Ridge

Pyrenees

Alps   EUROPE

Vesuvius

Olympus

Atlas

AFRICA

Kenya

Kilimanjaro

Urals

ASIA

Himalayas

K2

Everest

Fuji

Mid-Indian Ridge

Krakatoa

AUSTRALASIA

| 0 | 2,000 | 4,000 | miles |
| 0 | 2,000 4,000 | 6,000 | kilometres |

- • Mountains
- ▲ Volcanoes
- ■ Ocean ridges
- ■ Mountain ranges

This map shows the world's main mountain ranges and a selection of individual mountain peaks.

MOUNTAINS UNDER THE SEA

Mountains that rise from the seabed are sometimes called **seamounts**. Like mountains on land, they can occur in ranges or on their own. One of the biggest undersea mountain ranges is the Mid-Atlantic Ridge, which runs down the middle of the Atlantic Ocean. Sometimes, the peaks of undersea mountains stick out of the sea and form islands. The islands of Iceland, Ascension and the Azores are all parts of the Mid-Atlantic Ridge that rise above sea level.

LOCATION FILE

EASTER ISLAND

Easter Island is a tiny island in the Pacific Ocean, more than 2,000 km from the nearest land. Although the island itself is small, in fact it's just the tip of a giant volcano that rises nearly 3,000 m from the seabed. The volcano has not erupted since people settled on the island around 1,500 years ago.

MAKING MOUNTAINS

Mountains are made when part of the hard, rocky crust that covers the Earth moves upwards. This can happen in various ways. Most types of mountains – fold, fault, dome, and volcanic – get their names from the ways in which they were formed. The formation of mountains is called **orogenesis**.

FOLD MOUNTAINS

The Earth's outer crust is made up of huge sections called **tectonic plates**, fitted together like a jigsaw. They move very slowly, floating on the **magma** (molten rock) that's inside the Earth. Sometimes the plates push against each other, and their edges are slowly forced up into massive folds and wrinkles – or mountains. Most of the Earth's large mountain ranges, including the Himalayas, the Andes, the Alps and the Rockies, were formed in this way.

FAULT-BLOCK MOUNTAINS

Fault-block mountains are made when a huge block of rock separates from the rest of the Earth's crust, and is pushed upwards or sinks downwards.

BULGING DOMES

Dome mountains are a type of mountain made when magma – the hot molten rock under the Earth's crust – pushes upwards into softer overlying rocks, then cools and hardens. The weather then wears away the softer material. The Adirondacks in New York State, USA, and the mountains of the Lake District in England formed in this way and were worn away by **glaciers** during the last ice age.

Fold mountains form when the Earth's crust folds, or buckles, under pressure when two land masses push together.

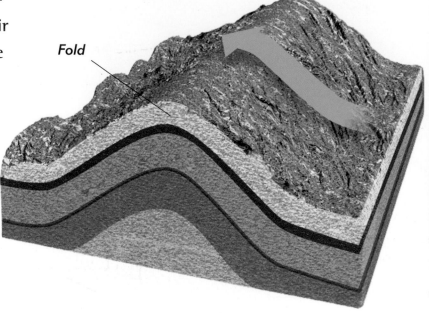

Fold

Fault-block mountains form when a section of the Earth's crust separates from the crust around it, and rises or sinks.

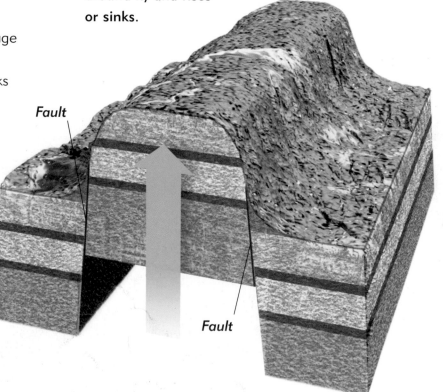

Fault

Fault

VOLCANIC ERUPTIONS

Fold mountains and fault-block mountains take millions of years to form, but a volcano can grow quickly – sometimes in just a few weeks. Volcanoes happen when magma from inside the Earth erupts (bursts) through the crust, and cools and hardens into rock. Volcanoes are common at places where tectonic plates meet. For example, there are lots of volcanoes in the Andes mountain range, where one plate pushes underneath another. Volcanoes can also form individually in areas where the Earth's crust is weak and magma can push through. You can find out more about volcanoes on pages 12–13.

You can find out more about volcanoes on pages 12–13.

LOCATION FILE

BIRTH OF A VOLCANO

In Mexico in 1943, a farmer named Dominic Pulido noticed a strange crack in one of his cornfields. Hot ash and lava started to come out of it, forming a cone shape. Within two months the new volcano, named Paricutin, was over 300 m high. Today Paricutin (below), which has stopped erupting, is a 424 m-high cone covering an area of over 25 km^2.

LOCATION FILE

THE FOLDED HIMALAYAS

The Himalayas are a classic example of fold mountains. They first started to grow about 50 million years ago, when the plate carrying India pushed against the rest of Asia. The two land masses squeezed together and crumpled up into a massive mountain range.

The sharp peaks of the Himalayas (below) were made by the folding of the Earth's crust.

HOW MOUNTAINS CHANGE

They might look solid and permanent, but mountains are changing all the time – even those that formed many millions of years ago. While the Earth's plates keep pushing mountains upwards, their peaks change shape as they erode (wear down) over time.

PUSHING UP

The tectonic plates that make up the Earth's crust are still moving very slowly – about as fast as your fingernails grow. That means that as the plates push together, some mountain ranges, such as the Himalayas and the Alps, are still growing. Mount Everest, for example, increases in height by at least 1 cm every year.

The Matterhorn, in the Swiss Alps, is famous for its unusual shape. The Alps formed as fold mountains when Italy and Europe pushed together. Glaciers then carved away the sides of the Matterhorn, giving it its 'horn' shape.

WEARING DOWN

Erosion happens when wind, rain and other forces wear rock and soil away. Because of their cold, harsh weather and steep, exposed slopes, mountains erode faster than the land around them. Gradually, a typical fold mountain wears down from a pointed peak into a smooth, rounded bump. The eroded material falls down into valleys, and rivers wash it away towards the sea, to become, finally, part of the seabed. Over millions of years, rocks that make up the Earth's crust move around in a cycle, being constantly pushed up and then eroded away. Geologists (scientists who study rocks and **landforms**) call this cycle the erosion cycle.

WHAT CAUSES EROSION?

Here are some of the things that can cause erosion on mountains.

• Wind blows soil and small rocks away.

• Rain washes soil down steep slopes.

• Ice expands as it freezes, cracking rocks into smaller pieces which can then be blown or washed away. Glaciers – huge, moving rivers of ice – carve valleys in mountainsides.

• Animals wear down tracks and dig burrows, dislodging rocks and soil.

• Humans erode mountains by wearing away paths and scrambling over rocks.

KRAKATOA

In 1883, Krakatoa, an island volcano in Indonesia, exploded so spectacularly that most of the mountain was blown away. Ash from the eruption landed as far as 6,000 km away, and more than 36,000 people were killed – mostly by the **tsunamis** (massive waves) the explosion caused.

This is Half Dome in California, USA. Its dome shape was probably made by underground magma (molten rock) pushing up through other rocks. Over time, the surrounding rocks eroded away, and glaciers flowing down the valley scraped away half of the dome.

SUDDEN CHANGES

Sometimes erosion eats away at a mountain peak until a huge chunk of rock falls off, giving the mountain a new shape almost overnight. Volcanic mountains can also change shape very suddenly, building up pressure inside until they are blown apart in a massive explosion. This happened to Mount St Helens, in Washington State, USA, in 1980. For several weeks magma built up inside the mountain, making it bulge on one side, and there were several small eruptions and earthquakes. Finally, on 18 May, the whole side of the mountain blew off. It was the biggest volcanic eruption in the history of the USA. Fifty-seven people were killed, and a huge area of farmland and forest was destroyed.

Small eruptions like this one still take place at the remains of Krakatoa in Indonesia.

VOLCANOES

Volcanoes are mountains that are formed when magma from inside the Earth bursts, or erupts, through the Earth's crust. A volcano can erupt many times. Each time, more magma comes out and builds up around the volcano, making it bigger and bigger.

INSIDE A VOLCANO

Most volcanoes are cone-shaped, because they are formed by rock and ash heaping up around the spot where the magma breaks through the Earth's crust. The magma moves up through a channel in the middle of the volcano, known as the vent. Sometimes smaller channels, called dykes, develop off the main vent. Once magma leaves a vent or a dyke and flows out of the volcano, it is known as lava.

ACTIVE, DORMANT OR EXTINCT ?

If a volcano is **active**, it means it erupts regularly. Stromboli in Italy and Arenal in Costa Rica are examples of active volcanoes that erupt almost every day. A **dormant** volcano, such as Haleakala in Hawaii, is one that hasn't erupted for a long time but could erupt again. An **extinct** volcano is one that volcanologists (volcano scientists) think will never erupt again.

HOT SPOTS AND THE RING OF FIRE

Volcanoes often occur near the edges of the Earth's tectonic plates. This is because the Earth's crust is more likely to be cracked there. Most of the world's active volcanoes are found in a ring around the Pacific Ocean, which lies on top of one big plate called the Pacific plate. This ring of volcanic activity is called the 'Ring of Fire'.

However, volcanoes can occur in the middle of plates too. They may form where there is an area of extra-hot magma, called a 'hot spot', under the Earth's crust.

The remains of Mount St Helens, in the USA, which exploded in a massive volcanic eruption in 1980. You can see another mountain, Mount Rainier, in the background.

LOCATION FILE

INNER-CITY VOLCANO

In Edinburgh in Scotland, UK, a castle stands on top of a giant rock in the middle of the city. The rock is actually a volcanic plug – the cooled, hardened vent of an ancient, extinct volcano. After the plug formed, the rest of the mountain was eroded away, leaving a solid rock column.

Edinburgh's Castle Rock, formed from the plug of an extinct volcano.

FACT FILE

FAMOUS VOLCANOES

NAME	PLACE	WHY IS IT FAMOUS?
Vesuvius	Italy	Erupted in AD 79, destroying the town of Pompei.
Fuji	Japan	Famous for its beauty, this volcano is regarded as sacred.
Mount St Helens	USA	Blew apart in a massive eruption in 1980.
Mauna Loa	Hawaii	Measured from the seabed, this is the biggest volcano in the world.
Ojos del Salado	Chile	At 6,885 m, it's the world's highest volcano measured from sea level.

STUDYING MOUNTAINS

Studying mountains involves a lot of guesswork. You can't cut a mountain in half to see how it's made, or go back in time to see when an extinct volcano last erupted. Instead, most mountain scientists think up theories (ideas about how things work) based on looking at mountain shapes and rocks and taking careful measurements.

LOOKING AT SHAPES

Scientists can work out a lot about a mountain from the way it looks. If it's smooth, rounded and worn away, it's probably very old, while mountains that formed more recently are sharp and jagged (see page 10). Other shapes can hold clues about different types of erosion. For example, long, deep, U-shaped mountain valleys were formed by glaciers – rivers of ice that move slowly down a mountain, pushing rock and soil out of the way. If a mountain has glacial valleys, it means that it was shaped during one of the Earth's ice ages, when the weather was much colder and icier than it is now.

LAYERS OF ROCK

A lot of the Earth's rock is made up of layers called **strata**. They were formed long ago when layers of mud or sand settled onto the land or seabed. Over time they were compressed (squashed) down into different types of hard rock. In places where the Earth's crust has been pushed up into mountains, rock strata can act as a record of the past. Patterns in the strata show how rock has moved, broken or folded, while fossils trapped in the layers can reveal when the rocks were formed.

These rocks in Yukon, Canada are made up of dozens of rock layers, or strata. When the layers formed they were horizontal, but movements in the Earth's crust have tilted and pushed them up.

MOUNTAIN SCIENTISTS

Here are some of the different types of scientists you might bump into on a mountain walk.

• GEOLOGISTS study rocks and how they are made.

• GEOMORPHOLOGISTS study the way the Earth changes – for example when mountains are made.

• PALAEONTOLOGISTS study fossils, which can give clues about how old mountain rocks are.

• VOLCANOLOGISTS (right) study volcanoes and predict volcanic eruptions.

VOLCANO SCIENCE

As well as studying how volcanoes were formed and how they work, volcanologists try to predict eruptions. They measure movements in the ground to see if pressure is building up inside a volcano, and collect material from active volcanoes' craters. Poisonous gases, flying rocks and lava flows sometimes cost volcanologists their lives. However, volcanologists also save many thousands of lives by warning when big eruptions will take place.

JAMES HUTTON

James Hutton (1726-1797) is often called 'the father of geology'. From studying rocks in Scotland where he lived, he realized that landforms such as mountains were formed through natural processes and changed over time. His ideas became the basis for much of modern Earth science.

MAPPING MOUNTAINS

Mapping means representing real-life landscapes on a flat piece of paper – a map. Mountains are hard to map for two main reasons. Firstly, they are remote and difficult to travel over, so taking all the right measurements is hard work. Secondly, they stick up from the ground, so cartographers (map-makers) have to find ways to show them in two dimensions.

HOW HIGH?

The height of a mountain – or any tall object – can be measured using triangulation, a kind of simple maths to do with triangles. If you know the length of one or more sides of a triangle, and two of its angles, you can work out the lengths of the other sides. Triangulation has been used for centuries to calculate mountain heights, but it is not always accurate.

Modern triangulation systems use lasers to get very accurate measurements. But different teams still get different results, and people still disagree about the heights of mountains.

Another way to measure altitude (height above sea level) is with a barometer, which measures air pressure. This works because air pressure drops as you get higher up, but since weather affects air pressure too, barometers are not always perfectly accurate.

The diagram below shows how triangulation measurements are taken and calculated.

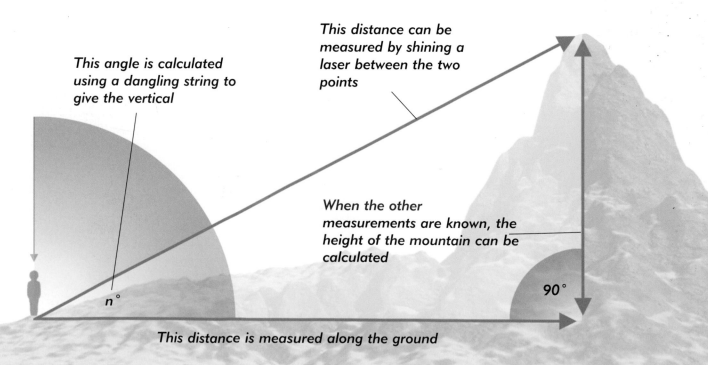

This angle is calculated using a dangling string to give the vertical

This distance can be measured by shining a laser between the two points

When the other measurements are known, the height of the mountain can be calculated

$n°$

$90°$

This distance is measured along the ground

MOUNTAINS ON MAPS

To show hills and mountains on a flat map, cartographers use **contour lines**. A contour line is a continuous line marking a particular height. For example, a map could have a contour line at every 10 m of altitude. The closer the lines are together, the steeper the real-life slope is.

SATELLITES AND COMPUTERS

Today many maps are made using **remote sensing**. It works by using **satellites orbiting** the Earth to photograph and measure landscapes. On the ground, **GPS** (Global Positioning System) equipment exchanges signals with satellites, allowing people to work out exactly where they are. This helps us to collect much more accurate information for making maps. We can also make 3D maps using computerized **GIS** (Geographic Information System) technology. It can display an image of a mountainous landscape which can be viewed from any angle.

A mountaineer with his tent and sleeping bag halfway up K2, now officially measured to be the world's second-highest mountain.

 LOCATION FILE

CONFUSING K2

K2 in the Himalayas is the second-highest mountain in the world, but at one point it was thought to be the highest. In 1987 a British team measured the mountain and got a result of 8,851 m – higher than Mount Everest. Debate raged until new measurements were taken in 1996. K2's official height is now 8,611 m.

MOUNTAIN ZONES

A big mountain can contain many different landscapes and climates. Near the bottom the surroundings are similar to a lowland area, with forests (except in polar regions) and gentle slopes. As you climb higher, and the weather gets colder, the trees give way to meadows, steep rocky slopes, and finally snow and ice. Because of this, geographers divide mountains into several different levels, or zones, each with its own landscape and vegetation (plant life).

TROPICAL OR TEMPERATE?

Although most big mountains have zones, the zones are different in different parts of the world. In hot, tropical places near the Equator, mountains have hot, wet rain forests or hot, dry grasslands near the bottom, with bamboo, flowering plants and moorland higher up. Mountains in cooler temperate regions, such as the Alps, have **deciduous** forests lower down, **evergreen** forests higher up, and rocky meadows near the top.

THE TREELINE

On big mountains, there is usually a line known as the treeline, above which very few trees can grow. This is partly because it's too cold and windy for them. It's also because not much soil can cling to the steep, rocky slopes high up a mountain, so there's nothing for tree roots to hold on to.

This diagram shows the zones of a mountain, on the left as in a tropical region, and on the right as in a temperate region.

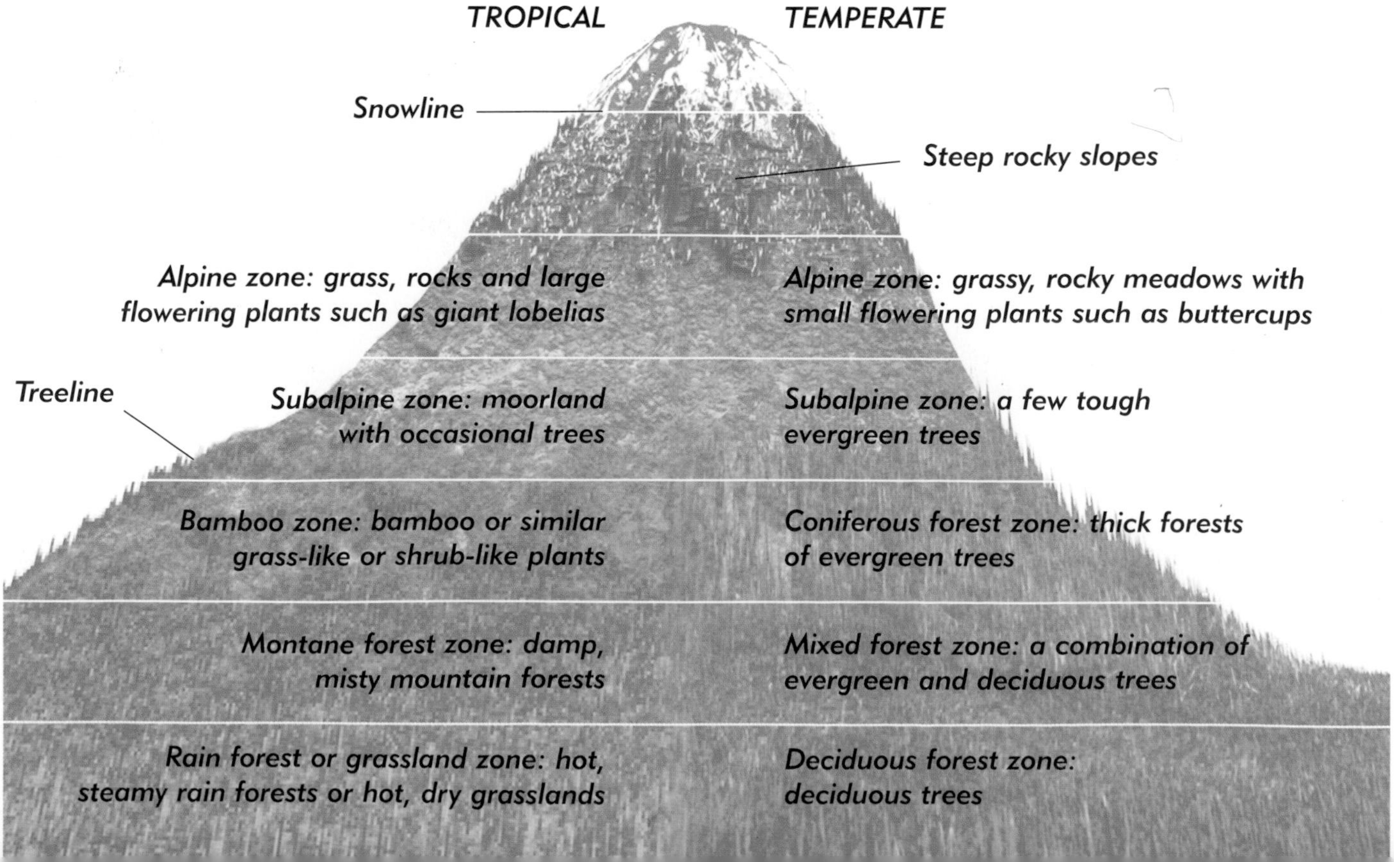

TROPICAL   TEMPERATE

Snowline

Steep rocky slopes

Alpine zone: grass, rocks and large flowering plants such as giant lobelias

Alpine zone: grassy, rocky meadows with small flowering plants such as buttercups

Treeline

Subalpine zone: moorland with occasional trees

Subalpine zone: a few tough evergreen trees

Bamboo zone: bamboo or similar grass-like or shrub-like plants

Coniferous forest zone: thick forests of evergreen trees

Montane forest zone: damp, misty mountain forests

Mixed forest zone: a combination of evergreen and deciduous trees

Rain forest or grassland zone: hot, steamy rain forests or hot, dry grasslands

Deciduous forest zone: deciduous trees

In this photo, you can see three mountain zones clearly. The alpine meadow, covered in grass, flowers and occasional rocks, is in the foreground. Higher up you can see the rocky slopes, and above them the icy mountain peak.

SNOW AND ICE

The tops of very high mountains, wherever they are in the world, are permanently covered with snow and ice. The area where it begins is called the snowline. Many mountains, such as those in the Alps, are completely covered by snow in winter.

CHANGING RIVERS

The headwaters, or starting points, of most big rivers are in mountain areas. A river begins as a small, cold, clear mountain stream, tumbling down the rocky mountainside and over waterfalls. As more streams flow into it the stream gets wider and becomes a river. As the slopes flatten out, the river forms loops and winding curves on its way to the sea.

LOCATION FILE

THE ZONES OF MOUNT EGMONT

Mount Egmont (left), also called Mount Taranaki, is a dormant volcano in New Zealand. Its neat cone shape shows off several mountain zones very clearly. This picture shows the mountain in summer. In winter it is completely covered in snow and ice.

Mount Egmont, New Zealand.

MOUNTAIN WILDLIFE

Like all wildlife, the plants and animals that live on mountains are adapted (suited) to their **habitats**, or surroundings. Because mountain zones create several different mountain habitats, different types of wildlife are found at different levels.

KEEPING WARM

Mountains are cold and windy, and there's not much shelter. To keep warm, many mountain animals have extra-thick hair or fur. Yaks in the Himalayas have two layers of hair: a thick, windproof outer coat, and a soft, fluffy layer underneath. Snow leopards and snowshoe hares have fur not only all over their bodies, but on the soles of their feet too. Many animals, including wildcats and birds such as snow finches, can fluff up their fur or feathers to trap a layer of warm air around their bodies. Even some mountain plants, such as the alpine silverleaf phacelia, have 'fur' to protect them from the cold.

FINDING FOOD

Food can be scarce in the mountains, especially in winter, so animals have to be good at finding it. Pikas – small furry animals similar to rabbits – collect grass in the summer, then dry it in the sun and store it to eat in winter. Lammergeiers (a type of vulture) feed on the bodies of goats and sheep that have died falling from steep rocks. Small birds called wallcreepers have special beaks for picking insects out of cracks between rocks, while Dall sheep can survive on a winter diet of lichen, moss and frozen grass.

These salmon are leaping up a waterfall in a mountain river in order to make their way back to the mountain stream where they were born. There they will breed, then die.

MOUNTAIN ANIMAL FACTS

To survive in mountain weather and terrain, mountain animals have to be tough. Here are some of their amazing feats:

• Bar-headed geese fly right over the tops of the Himalayas 9,000 m up – as high as an airliner.

• Jumping spiders have been found living in the snow 7,000 m up on Mount Everest.

• Big rocks and crags don't get in a cougar's way. It can jump more than 5 m straight upward.

• Wild salmon can leap 3.5 m out of the water, allowing them to jump over waterfalls as they swim up mountain streams.

• The mountain iguana can survive with a body temperature of only 1.5 °C – just above freezing.

PLANTS ON TOP

Mountain plants such as alpine forget-me-nots and dwarf willows are usually stockier than their cousins in lowland areas, with thicker stems and shorter branches. By clinging close to the ground they avoid being damaged or blown away by mountain winds.

Above **Snow leopards live in high mountains in Asia, such as the Himalayas. This one is walking through deep snow.**

Below **A Japanese macaque, also known as a snow monkey, warming itself in a natural hot spring.**

MONKEY MOUNTAIN

On the slopes of the Shiga Kogen volcano in Japan, Japanese macaques (a type of monkey) have found a brilliant way to keep warm. They spend their days sitting in hot springs that bubble up between the hot underground volcanic rocks.

MOUNTAIN ECOSYSTEMS

An **ecosystem** means a habitat and all the plants and animals that live in it together. Plants and animals eat each other and depend on each other to survive, so if one animal disappears from an ecosystem, it affects the others too. A whole mountain can be seen as one big ecosystem. Each zone, such as an alpine meadow or a tropical cloudforest, also has its own smaller ecosystem.

FOOD CHAINS AND WEBS

In the wild, animals survive by eating plants or other animals. One species eats another, and in turn is eaten by another, forming a sequence known as a food chain. Plants are always at the bottom of a food chain, with large hunting animals, such as big cats, at the top. A food web is a complicated system containing many interconnected food chains. Each animal in an ecosystem, such as a mountain forest, has its own place, or **niche**, in the food web.

CHANGING SURROUNDINGS

In an ecosystem, living things have to fit in with their surroundings in order to survive. When the weather and seasons change, plants and animals have to change too. Brown bears, for example, eat different foods in different seasons – such as eggs in spring, salmon that breed in mountain rivers in summer, and berries in the autumn. Many animals (such as bears and marmots) spend the freezing cold mountain winters hibernating in a cosy den or burrow. Hibernation is a kind of deep winter sleep, during which an animal doesn't need to eat.

West Caucasian turs live in the Caucasus Mountains. In summer, they feed high up on the mountain slopes. In winter, they move lower down to nibble the leaves of trees and bushes.

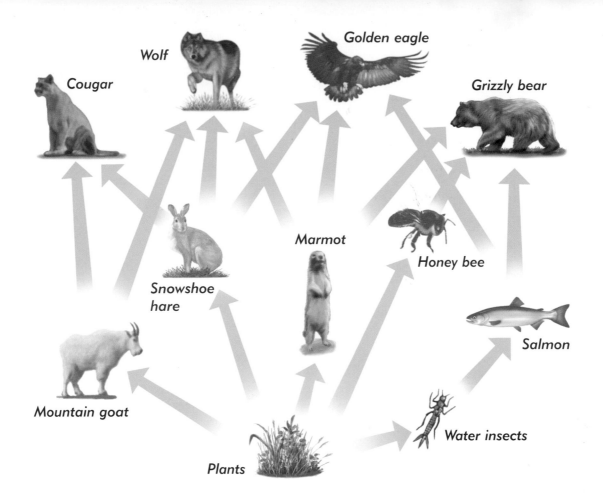

Cougar

Wolf

Golden eagle

Grizzly bear

Snowshoe hare

Marmot

Honey bee

Salmon

Mountain goat

Plants

Water insects

This diagram shows a simplified version of a food web in a North American mountain forest. Each arrow points from something that is eaten to an animal that eats it.

LIVING TOGETHER

While some living things in an ecosystem feed on each other, some help each other to survive. This kind of teamwork between two living things is called **symbiosis.** Lichens, which cling to high mountain rocks where few plants can survive, are actually made up of two living things, a fungus and an alga, in symbiosis. The fungus, a type of living thing similar to a mushroom, surrounds the alga, protecting it and keeping it damp. Meanwhile the alga, a type of tiny plant, uses sunlight to make food for both itself and the fungus.

FACT FILE

FOOD WEB LEVELS
Ecologists (scientists who study ecosystems) divide living things into different types, depending on their position in the food web.

• CONSUMERS Consumers is another word for 'eaters'. Animals that eat plants are called primary consumers. Animals that eat other animals are called secondary consumers.
• PRODUCERS Plants are called producers because they make (or produce) food using sunlight.
• DECOMPOSERS These include mushrooms and bacteria. They feed on dead plants and animals and help them to decompose (rot) and break down into chemicals that end in the soil. This makes food for plants, and so the cycle begins again.

MOUNTAIN WEATHER

Mountains have very extreme weather: gale-force winds, freezing temperatures and lots of rain and snow. This is partly because the shape of a mountain changes the weather around it, creating its own local climate.

THE HIGHER, THE COLDER

You might think the top of a mountain would be warmer than the bottom, since it's nearer the Sun. In fact it's much colder – so cold that even at the Equator, very high mountains such as 5,895 m-high Kilimanjaro in Tanzania always have snow and ice on their peaks.

There are several reasons for this. Firstly, higher up in the atmosphere, the air is thinner, and can't hold as much heat. Secondly, the sun hits mountain slopes at an angle, instead of directly from above, so its heating power is less concentrated. Lastly, rocky, icy mountain tops reflect heat away, instead of absorbing it like soil and plants do.

RAIN CATCHERS

As air approaches a mountainside, it is forced upwards. As it rises, the air gets colder, the water in it **condenses** to form clouds, and rain or snow falls. Because of this, mountains are often very rainy, especially on the side nearest the sea where the arriving air is moist and many clouds form. Sometimes, clouds cannot get past a mountain range. They drop all their rain on one side, and a desert, called a rainshadow desert, forms on the other side.

This illustration shows how a mountain range can force clouds to form, and rain or snow to fall.

Air cools as it rises

Water vapour in the air condenses and forms clouds. Water falls as rain.

Moist air blows in from sea

Ocean

Far side of the mountain receives very little rain and is called a rainshadow desert

COSTA RICA CLOUDFOREST

In Monteverde, Costa Rica, the mountain forests, called cloudforests, are continually shrouded in wet, misty clouds. The air is so damp that every surface is covered with mosses and air plants. Instead of sucking up water through roots, they soak it up from the air.

A cloudforest in Costa Rica.

WHY SO WINDY?

In lowland areas trees, hills and buildings slow wind down, but high up in the atmosphere winds can move much faster. When they hit a high mountain, especially above the treeline, the winds blast it with full force. On top of this, wind speeds up even more as it is channelled around and over mountain peaks.

FACT FILE

MOUNTAIN WEATHER FACTS

• The average temperature on top of Mount Everest is about –27 °C. It can drop to –60 °C. At sea level in nearby Dhaka, the average temperature is 25 °C.

• Mount Washington in New Hampshire, USA is one of the world's windiest peaks. The wind there averages 70 kph, and can gust to 370 kph.

• The heaviest snowfall ever measured in a single day hit mountains in Colorado, USA in April 1921, when 190 cm of snow fell.

• If a lot of snow falls on a mountaintop, it can collect into ice and flow slowly down the mountain as a glacier.

This glacier in Norway has reached the foot of the mountains and is flowing into the sea.

DANGERS AND DISASTERS

Mountains can be deadly killers. The combination of steep slopes, sheer cliffs, thick forests and bad weather make it easy to get lost or injured. Because mountains are often remote and unpopulated, it's hard to get help if you do run into trouble. Mountains can also be dangerous to those living at the bottom of them. Thousands and thousands of people have lost their lives in volcanic eruptions, mudslides and avalanches.

FEELING THE COLD

Cold is one of the biggest dangers facing mountaineers. Below a temperature of about −5 °C, body tissues can freeze, causing frostbite. Frostbite can damage noses, fingers and toes so badly that they sometimes have to be cut off. Even more dangerous is hypothermia, which happens when your whole body gets too cold.

DANGEROUS DROPS

Mountains are full of places where it's easy to fall. As well as steep slopes, loose rocks, cliffs and crags, high mountains have crevasses – deep cracks in glacier ice that can open up at any time. Mountaineers use special ladders to get across crevasses, but even the most experienced climbers sometimes fall down them.

AVALANCHE!

An avalanche happens when a mass of snow slips off a mountain. Avalanches can kill skiers and climbers caught in their path, and can even engulf whole villages. They are sometimes triggered by skiers disturbing the snow, but they can also happen by themselves.

LOCATION FILE

DEADLY EVEREST

More than 150 climbers have lost their lives climbing Mount Everest. The worst disaster happened on 10 May 1996, when several groups were trying to reach the summit at the same time. A sudden storm blew over and eight people were killed trying to make their way back down to safety.

The famous British mountaineer Alison Hargreaves, pictured on Mount Everest in 1995. She died later that year during an ascent of another mountain, K2.

This car was caught in a mountain mudslide in Boulder Creek, USA.

 FACT FILE

MOUNTAIN DISASTERS
This table lists some of the deadliest mountain disasters in history.

DATE	PLACE	DISASTER
1883	Krakatoa, Indonesia	Volcanic eruption caused tsunamis that killed 36,000 people.
1902	Mt Pelee, Martinique	30,000 were killed by being buried under volcanic ash.
1985	Ruiz, Colombia	Eruption melted ice, causing mudflows that killed 25,000 people.
1919	Kelut, Indonesia	Rock and mud flowing from the volcano claimed 5,000 lives.
1963	Alps, Italy	Vaiont Dam overflowed when the unstable hillside collapsed into the reservoir; 3,000 people died in floods.

ERUPTIONS AND MUDFLOWS

We can predict some volcanic eruptions, but others still happen unexpectedly, causing major disasters. As well as flinging out rock, ash and red-hot lava, volcanoes can cause massive mudflows, which often claim more lives than the eruption itself. This happens when a thick layer of ash coats a steep slope and is later saturated by heavy rain; the mudflow happens some time after the eruption.

MOUNTAIN RESOURCES

What do we get from mountains? As well as being beautiful and providing fun for tourists (see page 38), mountains contain a range of natural resources, such as minerals, energy and living things, that humans can collect and make use of.

MOUNTAIN MINERALS

Most mountains are made by huge movements in the Earth's crust. As well as pushing rock up to form mountains, these forces squeeze rocks or heat them up, forming valuable minerals such as emeralds, and rocks such as marble. The upheaval of the Earth's crust in mountain areas brings deposits of gold and other minerals nearer to the Earth's surface, so mountains are a great place to find precious stones and metals. We also collect huge amounts of other rock, such as granite, sandstone and limestone, from mountains to use in building.

DOWNHILL POWER

Mountains can make electricity too. When water flows down mountains in rivers, it holds a store of energy. We can convert this energy into electricity by building dams and using the flow of water to turn turbines. This is called **hydroelectric power** or HEP, and it is used a lot in mountainous countries such as Canada, Zaire and Norway. Over 90 per cent of Norway's energy comes from HEP.

A hydroelectric dam and power plant on the Kootenay River in the Rocky Mountains in Canada.

Chinchillas come from the high Andes mountains in northern Chile. Their fur is among the thickest and softest in the world. Each of a chinchilla's hair follicles has up to 60 hairs growing from it, instead of one as in most furry animals.

ANIMAL PRODUCTS

Because it is so thick and warm, hair or wool from mountain animals is often used to make luxury fabrics for humans to wear. For example, cashmere and pashmina wool come from Asian species of mountain goats. For a long time, humans have trapped other mountain animals, such as chinchillas and snow leopards, for their skins and fur. Many of these species are now protected by law to try to stop them from becoming extinct (see page 44).

FACT FILE

MOUNTAIN MATERIALS

See if you can find any of these items, which may have come from mountain areas, in your house or local area.

• PUMICE STONE Used for rubbing dead skin off your feet, pumice stone is made of cooled, hardened lava from volcanoes.

• EMERALDS Emeralds are green gemstones that are often found in mountain areas.

• ALUMINIUM FOIL Made from bauxite, a mineral mined from mountains in Jamaica and Brazil.

• MARBLE This mountain rock is used to make countertops and statues. It comes in many colours including pink, grey, black and white.

MOUNTAIN PEOPLE

Mountains are among the harshest, most remote places on Earth – yet some people manage to survive and make a living there. They usually live in small, isolated villages that are very difficult to reach from the outside world. In the past, unable to trade or communicate with outsiders, some mountain communities were totally self-sufficient and developed their own unique languages and customs.

SHELTERED SPOTS

Most mountain settlements and homes are found in sheltered mountain valleys. Here they are protected from the worst of the wind, and are close to a river or stream that can provide a water supply. Hardly anyone lives on the very top of a mountain, as it is too windy and exposed. The highest villages in the world are in the Himalayas, at altitudes of around 5,500 m – not much more than half the height of Mount Everest.

Porters carrying luggage for mountain trekkers in Nepal.

BUILT FOR ALTITUDE

The higher up a mountain you go, the less oxygen there is in the air. Above about 3,000 m, the lack of oxygen makes many lowlanders feel ill. But people who live permanently in high mountains are adapted, or suited, to low-oxygen conditions. They tend to be short and stocky, which helps them to resist the cold. They have extra red blood cells for carrying oxygen around their bodies, and some even have extra-large lungs. Andean highlanders, for example, have lungs up to 25 per cent bigger than a typical lowlander's lungs.

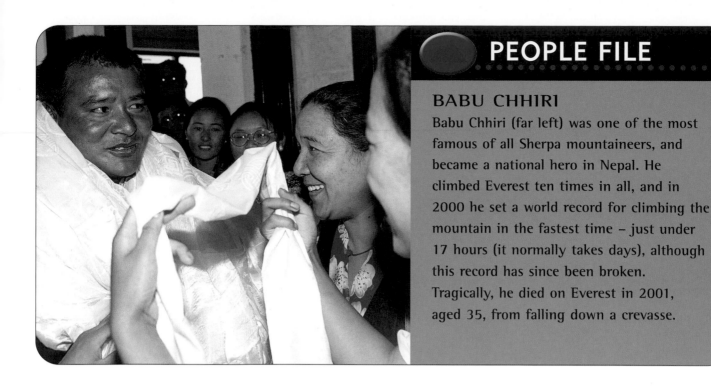

BABU CHHIRI

Babu Chhiri (far left) was one of the most famous of all Sherpa mountaineers, and became a national hero in Nepal. He climbed Everest ten times in all, and in 2000 he set a world record for climbing the mountain in the fastest time – just under 17 hours (it normally takes days), although this record has since been broken. Tragically, he died on Everest in 2001, aged 35, from falling down a crevasse.

EARNING A LIVING

Despite the poor soil and harsh weather, many mountain dwellers are farmers. They grow mountain crops such as coffee, or herd tough mountain animals, such as yaks, llamas or goats, that can forage for their own food. Another source of work for mountain people is acting as guides and porters for tourists and climbers who visit the mountains. This is especially true in the Himalayas, where the Sherpa people are renowned for their climbing skills and knowledge of the mountains.

MOUNTAINOUS NATIONS

Here are some of the world's most mountainous countries:
• NEPAL Sandwiched between India and China, tiny Nepal borders the highest Himalayan peaks.
• BOLIVIA Around 60 per cent of Bolivia's people live in the Andes mountains.
• ETHIOPIA The country is dominated by the huge fault mountains on either side of Africa's Great Rift Valley.
• IRAN Iran, in the Middle East, is mostly made up of mountains, surrounding a central plateau.
• SWITZERLAND In the middle of the Alps, Switzerland is the most mountainous country in Europe.
• JAPAN Japan is 90 per cent mountains.

A market in an Andean mountain village in Peru.

31

MOUNTAIN TOWNS

Most mountain settlements are small towns or villages. Their buildings tend to be low and squat, so they don't get damaged by high winds. Big cities need good communications routes and plenty of flat land for building, so cities in the mountains are quite rare.

HIGH-ALTITUDE HOMES

Mountain houses are designed to deal with wind, cold and heavy snow. They usually have small windows and big roofs that stick out a long way to stop snow from drifting up against the door. In parts of the Himalayas, traditional homes are built of mud bricks and have two storeys. While the people live upstairs, the lower floor is used as a stable for farm animals, and the warmth from their bodies helps to heat the house. In the Alps, the snow itself is used to keep homes warm. Many houses have rocks or small fences fixed to their roofs to keep the snow from sliding off. It acts like a layer of roof insulation to stop heat escaping from the house.

FACT FILE

CITIES ON TOP OF THE WORLD
These are some of the highest cities in the world:
• Wenquan in China is officially the world's highest city, at 5,100 m.
• La Paz in Bolivia, at 3,630 m, is the world's highest capital city.
• Potosi, another city in Bolivia, is even higher – 4,090 m.
• Leadville, Colorado, the highest city in the USA, has an altitude of 3,110 m.
• Lhasa, a city in Tibet, now ruled by China, is at 3,700 m.

MOUNTAIN TRANSPORT

How do you reach a mountain town? Some mountain slopes are so steep it's impossible to travel straight up them. Instead, mountain roads wind to and fro in a series of hairpin bends. This makes them less steep, but much longer – so even where there are roads, travel in the mountains can take a long time. Where there's only a rough, steep track, animals usually make the best transport. Yaks, llamas or mules can carry heavy loads, or human passengers, safely up and down the steepest mountainsides.

Snow-covered wooden chalets (mountain cottages) in Valais, Switzerland.

The ruins of the ancient Inca mountain
city of Machu Picchu.

SAFE IN THE MOUNTAINS

In the past, castles and fortified towns were built
on mountains to give them an advantage in case
of an attack. In Greece, for example, people living
in seaside towns often built another town in the
nearest mountains which they could retreat to if
invaders arrived.

LOCATION FILE

MACHU PICCHU
The ruined city of Machu Picchu is
2,400 m up in the Andes in Peru, South
America. Built by the Inca people in
the fifteenth century, it was probably an
outpost of the Inca civilization. It lay
deserted for more than 300 years, but
since being rediscovered in 1911 it has
become a major tourist attraction.

MOUNTAIN FARMS

Farming on a high mountain is no easy feat. The soil easily gets blown or washed away down the steep hillsides, and farm animals have to put up with freezing weather. Yet mountain farms provide a living for millions of mountain farmers around the world. Many of them are subsistence farmers – they grow just enough food to keep themselves and their families alive.

MOUNTAIN FARM ANIMALS

Mountain farm animals are bred from animals that live naturally at high altitudes, and so are used to the harsh conditions. In the Himalayas, farm yaks are related to the wild yaks that have lived there for millennia. Many mountain farmers also keep mountain sheep and goats. In the Andes, farmers breed alpacas and llamas for their wool, milk and meat, and some also keep guinea pigs, which are native to the Andes mountains, to use as food.

MOUNTAIN CROPS

Mountain farmers grow hardy crops that can cope with thin soil and cold, windy weather, and provide a regular supply of food. The most popular include barley, quinoa (a type of cereal crop) and potatoes. A few crop plants, such as coffee and some types of berries, grow best at high altitude, as do medicinal herbs such as the Indian gentian. Some specialist mountain farmers grow crops like these to sell.

A mountain farmer in India harvests coffee beans from a coffee bush. Most types of coffee grow best at high altitudes.

YAK FACTS

For isolated mountain farmers the best animals are those that have many different uses. The most useful of all is probably the yak (right). It provides:

- Milk for drinking and making into butter. The butter is used as lamp fuel.
- Meat, which can be eaten fresh or preserved by drying.
- Leather, used for making shoes and bags.
- Thick woolly hair, used to make rope, blankets and clothes.
- Dung, which can be dried and used as fuel.
- Heat from its body, used to heat homes.
- Transport for both people and goods.

These Mongolian farmers are milking their yaks at their summer grazing meadows.

TERRACES

Terraces are used on mountain farms around the world. They are steps dug into a hillside and supported with walls. This creates small areas of level land for farming on, and stops soil and water from being washed away.

Bolivian farmers in the countryside around La Paz, in the Andes, harvesting potatoes.

LOCATION FILE

UP AND DOWN

In the Swiss Alps, as in many mountain areas, farmers move their animals up the mountains in spring and summer to feed on the fresh young grass. In winter the animals are moved back down to lower altitudes to keep warm.

MOUNTAIN INDUSTRIES

In some parts of the world, mountains are home to huge industrial activity, especially mining the valuable stones and metals that mountains contain. Industries like these provide mountain people with jobs, but they can also scar mountains forever.

MOUNTAIN MINING

Mining is a huge mountain industry. It ranges from small-scale methods, such as **panning** for gold, which do not affect the landscape, to massive open-cast mining and quarrying operations. They involve bulldozing or blasting the mountainside open to gain access to the precious deposits. Some mountains have been changed forever by mining. At Potosi in Bolivia, for example, Cerro Rico (Rich Hill) has been mined so extensively for silver that the mountain is 300 m shorter than it used to be.

LOCATION FILE

THE MUZO MINE
The Andean town of Muzo, Colombia, is home to the world's biggest emerald mine. Besides the hundreds of miners who are officially employed at the mine, thousands of local people make a living by picking through the leftover dirt for emerald fragments. These emerald-hunters are known as *Guaqueros.*

Guaqueros search through leftover rubble and dust outside an emerald mine in Colombia, hoping to find valuable emerald scraps.

COTTAGE INDUSTRIES

A cottage industry is an industry that's carried out on a small scale at home, instead of by mass production in big factories. In mountain areas, where it's hard to build factories, cottage industries are very important. The most common are weaving and making clothes and leather goods, using the hair and skin of mountain farm animals such as sheep, yaks and goats. In the Atlas Mountains in North Africa, for example, women weave sheep's wool and goat hair into rugs which can be sold to tourists.

MOUNTAIN LOGGING

Logging – cutting down trees for their wood – happens wherever there are trees. It's more common in lowland areas where the wood is easily transported away, but as lowland forests get used up, loggers in some areas have moved to mountain forests instead. Logging can cause problems on hillsides as it leads to soil being washed away (see page 42).

Moroccan mountain weavers and rug-makers come to this market in the city of Marrakesh to sell their wares.

PEOPLE FILE

JAMES MARSHALL

In 1848, carpenter James Marshall was building a sawmill on the American River in Coloma, California, USA, when he found tiny grains of gold in the river water. Although he tried to keep it a secret, his discovery led to one of the biggest gold mining operations in history – the California Gold Rush. Millions of people flocked to the Californian mountains and millions of dollars worth of gold was extracted. John Marshall, however, never struck lucky again, and died in poverty.

MOUNTAIN TOURISM

Mountains attract millions of tourists every year. Their wild landscapes offer a chance to escape from busy cities and developed areas, and act as a playground for dozens of different sports and activities.

AMAZING VIEWS

People like to climb mountains for the challenge, but also for the view or to see amazing sights, such as a moving glacier or the crater of an active volcano. In Hawaii, for example, the Volcanoes National Park, where tourists can see lava flowing from Kilauea, the world's most active volcano, is the most popular tourist attraction in the state.

EXCITING SPORTS

Steep slopes, snow and wide open spaces mean mountains are the perfect place for exciting sports. The biggest mountain sport is skiing. Around the world, skiing resorts attract millions of tourists and employ millions of people every year. Other mountain sports include walking, climbing, snowboarding, white-water rafting and mountain biking, as well as several more extreme sports.

JOBS IN TOURISM

While it can be hard to find normal office jobs in mountain areas, tourism creates huge numbers of jobs doing things like teaching people to ski and rock-climb, leading guided walks, and working in hotels. A lot of these jobs are **casual work** and seasonal, but they still provide many people with an important income. In countries such as Canada, Switzerland, Nepal and Scotland, mountain tourism makes up an important part of the economy.

Tourists watch lava from a Hawaiian volcano flowing into the sea.

EXTREME SPORTS

Here are just a few of the more extreme and unusual mountain sports:

- CANYONING Wading, abseiling and swimming down the canyons and waterfalls of a mountain river.
- ZORBING or SPHEREING Rolling down a steep slope inside a giant inflatable plastic sphere.
- PARAGLIDING Jumping off high places using a parachute-like device to fly back to the valley floor.
- ICE CLIMBING Climbing up glaciers or frozen waterfalls.
- ZIPLINING Sliding along a cable strung between two high points.

Snowboarding (above) and skiing are the most popular mountain sports.

LOCATION FILE

ASPEN, COLORADO

In the 1930s Aspen, a run-down former mining town in the Rocky Mountains, had a population of just 700. Then, in 1935, it began to be developed for skiing. Today, it is one of the best-known skiing resorts in the world and is famous for its celebrity visitors. It has a permanent population of 7,000, which swells to over 40,000 during peak season, and is one of the USA's wealthiest towns.

MANAGING MOUNTAINS

Mountain areas can easily be damaged by too much industry, farming and tourism. Managing mountains means controlling the way mountain areas are developed, to try to preserve them and keep them clean.

MOUNTAIN DEVELOPMENT

People want to go to the mountains on holiday, to take part in skiing and other sports and to experience the natural beauty of a wilderness area. Many people also want to develop mountain areas in order to create jobs for local people. However, by building hotels, roads, ski-lifts, public toilets and so on, we are in danger of destroying the very untamed beauty that makes mountains attractive. So it is important to manage mountain development to preserve a balance between keeping wild areas wild, and making it possible to visit and enjoy them.

NATIONAL PARKS

A national park is an area of land that is set aside to protect it from damage and overdevelopment. Many mountain regions have been made into national parks to preserve them for the future. A typical national park has visitor facilities such as toilets, litter bins and marked trails, allowing people to visit a wild area while keeping damage and pollution to a minimum. There may also be park wardens who patrol the park and protect wildlife.

WHO OWNS MOUNTAINS?

Unlike lowland areas, mountains are usually not bought and sold as land. This is partly because they make poor farmland and are hard to build on. Instead, mountain areas are often owned by the governments of the countries they lie in, and it is up to these governments to make laws to keep mountains safe and protect their wildlife and landscapes.

LOCATION FILE

YELLOWSTONE

Yellowstone National Park, in northwestern USA, is the oldest national park in the world. It was founded in 1872 and has nearly 3 million visitors a year. It covers nearly a million hectares of mountainous territory and is home to mountain animals such as wolves, bighorn sheep and grizzly bears.

A park ranger at Yellowstone uses special equipment to check levels of air pollution in the park.

However, in many countries, especially those with civil wars such as Colombia and Afghanistan, mountain areas may be ruled by local clans or rebel groups. This makes it hard for governments to control and regulate mountain areas.

LOCATION FILE...

SCOTLAND'S CAIRNGORMS

The Cairngorm mountains in Scotland are an example of a mountain area that has been caught in a clash of conflicting interests. While developers wanted to build more and more skiing resorts and hotels to make money, environmentalists wanted to keep tourists out of some areas in case they disturbed rare mountain birds such as the golden eagle, snow bunting and capercaillie. To try to end this conflict, the Cairngorms were made into a national park in 2003.

A golden eagle, one of the rare mountain bird species that campaigners in the Cairngorms have fought to protect.

MOUNTAINS IN DANGER

Mountains might seem tough, but in fact mountain ecosystems are fragile and easily damaged, and many mountain areas are threatened by pollution and mismanagement.

STEEP SLOPES

One reason that mountains are so vulnerable is their steep slopes. The soil there is held in place by trees and plants. Methods such as terracing (see page 35) can keep soil from being washed away, but if a hillside is deforested (stripped of its trees) and then left bare, the soil can disappear within a few decades. This can harm whole mountain food webs, as animals depend on soil and plants for their food. It can also harm humans, as the steady washing away of soil over a long period pollutes rivers and depletes farmland. Sometimes loose rocks and soil may crash down the mountain in a landslide, flattening towns or blocking rivers and roads.

POLLUTION FROM FAR AWAY

Even mountains that are far away from towns and cities can be seriously affected by pollution. Chemical waste from cars and factories rises up into the atmosphere and makes rainwater acidic. Because clouds are especially likely to drop their rain on mountains (see page 24) mountain areas get the worst of this acid rain. It can damage forests and change the chemical balance of mountain lakes, killing the wildlife that lives there. On top of this, visitors to mountains can cause a pollution problem by leaving litter behind.

An aerial view of mountain forests in Washington State, USA. On the right, you can see where the forests have been cut down, leaving bare hillside and destroying the habitat of mountain forest animals.

Waste left on Mount Everest.

MESSY MOUNT EVEREST

Since it was first climbed in 1953 by Sir Edmund Hillary and Tenzing Norgay, Mount Everest has become a dumping ground. Hundreds of people have climbed to the top, and the route is now littered with plastic waste and used oxygen canisters. There are even dozens of frozen dead bodies. Since the year 2000, several climbing expeditions have gone to the mountain just to clean some of the litter up.

WILDLIFE IN DANGER

Mountain plants and animals are specially adapted for living in their high-altitude homes. If their habitats are damaged – for example if a mountain forest is chopped down for wood, or to make room for a ski slope – they have nowhere else to go and are in danger of dying out. Some mountain animals are also at risk from poachers who hunt them for their fur, horns or meat.

FACT FILE

ENDANGERED MOUNTAIN ANIMALS

Many mountain animals are endangered (at risk of dying out). Here are just a few of them:

• Snow leopards in the Himalayas are at risk from poachers and habitat loss.

• Mountain gorillas in central Africa are hunted for meat, and are also killed in wars and by viruses.

• Giant pandas in China are dying out because of deforestation of the mountain bamboo forests where they live.

• Kakapos – flightless parrots that live in mountain forests in New Zealand – have declined since humans took cats, dogs and other hunting animals there.

• Grizzly bears in the USA are endangered because so many have been killed to protect humans and livestock.

A rare wild giant panda.

CONSERVING MOUNTAINS

Today, although some mountain areas and plant and animal species are still in danger, governments and organizations around the world are making efforts to conserve (save) them.

PARKS AND RESERVES

National parks help to conserve mountains by keeping them safe from crimes (such as poaching, pollution and stealing eggs) and overdevelopment. Park rangers and wardens guard against poaching and control the numbers of tourists entering the park. Some countries also have special wildlife reserves, where one or more species of endangered animals can live in safety. However, managing mountain areas in this way is very expensive, and some poorer countries cannot afford to do it.

CONSERVATION LAWS

Governments can help to conserve mountains and other wild areas using laws. For example, hunting endangered wild animals such as snow leopards is now illegal in most countries. There are also laws that force developers to obtain planning permission before they can develop a mountain area into a tourist resort. If the development would damage the landscape or wildlife too much, permission can be denied. However, like all laws, these laws have to be enforced – and in remote mountain regions, that can be very difficult.

In Sweden, many forests are now sustainable, which means each tree that is cut down for timber is replaced.

RULES FOR VISITORS

Many national parks have rules for their visitors to protect the local landscape and wildlife. For example, asking tourists to stick to specially-built paths can make sure other parts of the mountain aren't eroded away by thousands of feet. Most parks also ask tourists not to start fires, leave litter or collect plants. At some times of year, certain areas of a national park may be closed to the public so that animals can be left alone to breed and raise their babies safely.

Right **A Nubian ibex with her calf.**

GLOSSARY

Active An active volcano is one that erupts regularly.

Adapt When a plant or animal species adapts, it changes over time to suit its habitat.

Altitude Height above sea level.

Casual work Work that isn't permanent, is often seasonal, and maybe comes by chance.

Condense To change from a gas (such as water vapour) into a liquid.

Contour lines Lines on a map that mark levels of altitude.

Deciduous Deciduous trees and shrubs shed their leaves in winter.

Dormant A dormant volcano has stopped erupting, but could erupt again one day.

Ecosystem A habitat and all the plants and animals that live in it.

Erosion Wearing away of rock and soil.

Evergreen Evergreen trees and shrubs keep their leaves all the year round.

Extinct If a plant or animal species is extinct, it has died out forever. An extinct volcano is one that will never erupt again.

GIS (Geographic Information System) Computer technology used for making and displaying maps.

Glacier A river of ice that inches slowly down a mountain, fed by the snow and ice that collects on top, or a sheet of ice covering a large area.

GPS (Global Positioning System) Technology that works out the positions of points on the globe using satellites.

Habitat The place where a plant or animal species lives, such as a forest or a mountain meadow.

HEP (Hydroelectric power) Power generated by harnessing the energy of water flowing downhill.

Landforms The different shapes land is formed into, such as mountains and valleys.

Magma Hot, molten rock inside the Earth.

Niche The unique role a plant or animal species has in its ecosystem.

Orbiting Moving around another object. For example, satellites orbit the Earth.

Orogenesis A scientific name for what happens when mountains are formed.

Panning Trying to find gold by swirling rocks and mud from a river around in a pan. If there is any gold, it sinks to the bottom.

Remote sensing Recording information about the Earth from far away, usually by using satellites.

Satellite A machine sent up into space to orbit the Earth. Some satellites are used to take photos of the Earth or record other geographical information.

Seamount A mountain under the sea.

Strata Layers found in rock.

Symbiosis When two plant or animal species live together in a way that helps both partners.

Tectonic plate One of the massive sections of rock that make up the Earth's crust.

Terrain A type of land with particular features. For example, mountain terrain can be very rocky and steep.

Tsunami A massive wave caused by movements in the Earth below the ocean floor, such as earthquakes or volcanic eruptions. Tsunamis can travel long distances across oceans before crashing onto the shore, where they often cause serious damage.

Wilderness Wild, undeveloped land.

FURTHER INFORMATION

WEBSITES TO VISIT

www.mountain.org/education/

The Learning about Mountains site is intended as a fun guide to mountains, and has links to other sites where you can see videos of mountain animals and listen to mountain musical instruments.
The Mountain Institute
1828 L Street NW, Suite 725
Washington, DC 20036, USA
Tel: +1 (202) 452 1636
Email: summit@mountain.org

www.enchantedlearning.com/subjects/volcano/activities.shtml

A set of information pages, activities and volcano experiments to try.
Enchanted Learning
PO Box 321, Mercer Island
WA 98040-0321, USA
Tel: +1 (206) 232-4880.
Email: info@EnchantedLearning.com

www.nps.gov/yell/home.htm

The official website of Yellowstone National Park, with pages of information on wildlife and geological features, plus games and activities.
Yellowstone National Park
PO Box 168
WY 82190-0168, USA
Visitor Information Tel: +1 (307) 344 7381
Email: yell_visitor_services@nps.gov

BOOKS TO READ

Horrible Geography: *Freaky Peaks* by Anita Ganeri
(Scholastic Children's Books, 2001)
Mapping Earthforms: *Mountains* by Catherine Chambers
(Heinemann Library, 2002)
Biomes Atlases: *Mountains and Highlands* by Tim Harris
(Raintree, 2004)
To the Top: The Story of Everest by Steven Venables
(Walker Books, 2003)
Endangered Mountain Animals by Dave Taylor
(Crabtree Publishing, 1992)

INDEX